HALSEY

TWO EXTRAORDINARY PEOPLE.

BILLIE EILISH

CONNECTED LIVES™

Ariana Grande | Camila Cabello

Ed Sheeran | Shawn Mendes

Halsey | Billie Eilish

John Legend | Michael Bublé

Kacey Musgraves | Maren Morris

Kane Brown | Sam Hunt

Kendrick Lamar | Travis Scott

Nicki Minaj | Cardi B

Photo credits: page 4: Rich Fury / iHeartMedia via Getty Images; page 5: Bryan Steffy via Getty Images; page 6: Astrid Stawiarz / Glamour via Getty Images; page 7: Joe Scarnici / Spotify via Getty Images; page 8: Doug Schneider Photography / Moment via Getty Images; page 10: Getty Images for Saks Fifth Avenue via Getty Images, Dzurag / iStock via Getty Images; page 12: Kevin Winter via Getty Images; page 13: Frazer Harrison via Getty Images; page 16: Adam Bettcher / iHeartMedia via Getty Images, Fermate / iStockphoto via Getty Images; page 17: Kevin Winter / Coachella via Getty Images; page 18: Frazer Harrison / iHeartMedia via Getty Images; page 19: Ilya S. Savenok / Glamour via Getty Images; page 20: Kevin Winter via Getty Images, Mutlu Kurtbas / iStock Unreleased via Getty Images; page 21: Jim Bennett via Getty Images; page 22: ozgurdonmaz / iStock Unreleased via Getty Images, Astrid Stawiarz / The Elvis Duran Z100 Morning Show via Getty Images; page 23: Emma McIntyre / KROQ/Entercom via Getty Images; page 24: Kevin Winter / iHeartMedia via Getty Images; page 25: Kaycco / iStockphoto via Getty Images; page 28: Jason Merritt via Getty Images; page 29: Getty Images for Live Nation via Getty Images; page 30: Kevin Winter / CBS Radio via Getty Images; page 32: Natalie Cass / popsugar via Getty Images; page 33: Ari Perilstein / ASCAP via Getty Images; page 35: Vivien Killilea / dick clark productions via Getty Images; page 36: Noam Galai via Getty Images; page 37: Kevin Winter / KROQ/Entercom via Getty Images; page 40: Kevin Winter via Getty Images; page 41: Rich Polk / iHeartMedia via Getty Images; page 42: Frazer Harrison / Coachella via Getty Images; page 43: Nicholas Hunt via Getty Images; page 44: Jason Kempin via Getty Images; page 45: Randy Shropshire / UNICEF USA via Getty Images; page 46: Brad Barket / H&M via Getty Images; page 47: Frazer Harrison / Coachella via Getty Images; page 49: Scott Legato / Live Nation via Getty Images, Jim Dyson via Getty Images; page 52: Brad Barket via Getty Images; page 53: Kevin Winter via Getty Images; page 56: Rick Kern / Samsung via Getty Images; page 58: Nicholas Hunt via Getty Images; page 59: Kevin Winter via Getty Images; page 60: Erika Goldring / Bud Light via Getty Images; page 61: Nicholas Hunt / Taste Of The NFL via Getty Images; page 62: Gustavo Caballero / iHeartMedia via Getty Images; page 63: Kevin Winter / Coachella via Getty Images; page 64: Leon Neal via Getty Images, Christopher Polk / MTV via Getty Images; background: Chris Wong / EyeEm via Getty Images; Halsey head shot: Dia Dipasupil via Getty Images; Billie Eilish head shot: Rich Fury via Getty Images

ISBN: 978-1-68021-791-9
eBook: 978-1-64598-077-3

Printed in Malaysia

24 23 22 21 20   1 2 3 4 5

TABLE OF CONTENTS

CHAPTER 1

EARLY LIFE

WHO IS HALSEY?

Halsey is a singer and songwriter. Her given name is Ashley Nicolette Frangipane. She was born on September 29, 1994, in Clark, New Jersey. The star still visits her home state. New Jersey is "like a little sister or a little brother that's annoying . . . but I love you still," the singer told Business Insider.

WHO IS BILLIE EILISH?

Singer and songwriter Billie Eilish was born on December 18, 2001. Her parents named her Billie Eilish Pirate Baird O'Connell. The singer was named after her grandfather Bill. "Pirate was going to be my middle name," she told the BBC in 2017. "But then my uncle had a problem with it because pirates are bad. Then Baird is my mother's name." Billie was born in Los Angeles, California.

Nicole Frangipane

THE FRANGIPANE FAMILY

Halsey's parents are Nicole and Chris. They had her very young. Both dropped out of college to raise their child. Nicole worked security at a hospital. Chris managed a car dealership. Halsey's mother is Italian and Hungarian. Her father is African American and Irish.

THE BAIRD O'CONNELL FAMILY

Billie's parents are Maggie Baird and Patrick O'Connell. They are both of Irish and Scottish descent. While working as actors in a play, the two met and fell in love. Maggie was in a famous comedy group called the Groundlings. Billie's parents were older than Halsey's parents when they had children. At that point, they stopped focusing on acting. Both did voice-over work, and Maggie taught trapeze classes. Patrick also worked at Mattel. He built displays for selling Barbie dolls.

Maggie Baird

WORKING-CLASS NEW JERSEY GIRL

Nicole and Chris changed jobs often when Halsey was a child. They sometimes had to work two jobs each. The family moved from town to town for work. "I grew up in a really chaotic household," Halsey told *Rolling Stone*. She changed schools nearly every year until the age of 13.

Edison, New Jersey

Highland Park, Los Angeles

A BOHEMIAN FAMILY

Billie is from an artistic family. Like Halsey, her childhood was not privileged. She was raised in Highland Park, Los Angeles. The singer says it was too dangerous to go outside after dark. "Automatically, people think you're from Beverly Hills. . . . Not at all. I grew up with no money at all. . . . I had one pair of shoes and a shirt," the star told the *Guardian*. Her parents still sleep in the living room of their two-bedroom bungalow.

SCHOOL DAYS

Halsey went to Warren Hills Regional High School. This is in Washington, New Jersey. It is a small town. The teenager took advanced placement (AP) classes and was a good student. However, she did not fit in. Halsey was more artistic than many of her classmates. Painting was a hobby. She designed the school yearbook too. At 14, Halsey was posting her paintings and other work on MySpace. The teen also worked at a music venue. There, she helped to book bands. In 2012, the future star graduated high school.

HOMESCHOOL

While Halsey went to many different schools, the Baird O'Connell children were homeschooled. Creativity and self-expression were important. Maggie explained to *Vogue*, "We homeschooled in a way that was interest-led and experiential. Nothing had a higher value than the other." Billie and her brother took art classes. They also went to museums. Her parents taught them math through cooking. Billie earned her GED when she was 15.

HOMESCHOOLED STARS

Homeschooled students are often academic high achievers. Many stars have been homeschooled. Some began homeschooling after they became stars, and others long before. Stars who were homeschooled include Justin Bieber, Emma Watson, Venus and Serena Williams, the Jonas Brothers, Christina Aguilera, and Ryan Gosling. Demi Lovato and Selena Gomez were even homeschooled together.

THE OLDER SISTER

The Frangipanes had two sons after Halsey. Sevian is four years younger than his famous sister. He enrolled at California State University, Northridge and plays golf. Halsey and Sevian are very close. She took him to the American Music Awards in 2016. Dante is the baby of the family. Like his sister, he is artistic. Halsey used her little brother's voice in her song "Good Mourning."

INDEPENDENT YOUNG STARS

Many stars leave school and home to start careers at a young age. Travis Scott left college to pursue rapping without telling his parents. R&B legend Mary J. Blige dropped out of high school. Piano-playing icon Billy Joel, pop-punk singer Avril Lavigne, and rap superstar Jay-Z did too.

Jay-Z

THE YOUNGER SISTER

Unlike Halsey, Billie is the youngest in her family. Finneas O'Connell is the singer's older brother. Born in 1997, Finneas is also a talented musician. He releases his own music under the name FINNEAS. Acting is also a talent of his. TV shows *Glee* and *Modern Family* are on his résumé. The siblings have always had a strong relationship. They work together even more than Halsey and Dante. "We're a pretty close-knit family to begin with so that's not really super new," Finneas told *Atwood Magazine*.

Finneas O'Connell

A DIFFERENT PATH

After high school, Halsey was accepted to the art school Rhode Island School of Design. However, her family could not afford it. Instead, she went to community college. Creative writing was her major. Feeling that it was a waste of time, she dropped out. Then the singer moved to New York City. It was against her parents' wishes. "They just didn't agree with a lot of things about me," she told *Rolling Stone*. Her parents stopped supporting her. Halsey's mental health suffered.

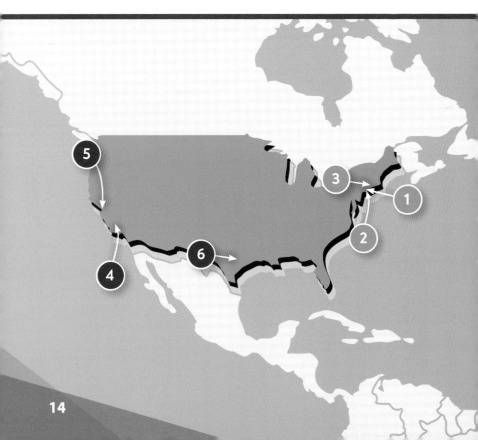

A SENSITIVE CHILD

While Halsey was independent, Billie needed her parents around. She slept in her parents' bed until she was ten. The star also has synesthesia. This is a condition where senses blend together. It affects Billie's life in good and bad ways. People and even songs are associated with colors, shapes, and smells. "'Bad Guy' is yellow, but also red, and the number seven," she told *Rolling Stone*.

HALSEY

1. **Clark, New Jersey:** This is the town where Halsey was born.
2. **Washington, New Jersey:** Halsey went to high school in this small town.
3. **New York City, New York:** Halsey moved here after leaving college to strike out on her own.

BILLIE EILISH

4. **Los Angeles, California:** Billie was born and raised in the Highland Park neighborhood.
5. **San Francisco, California:** Rickshaw Stop was the location of her first official concert.
6. **Austin, Texas:** SXSW was Billie's first festival performance. Her album had not been released yet.

CHAPTER 2

INTRO TO MUSIC

PIANO CAME FIRST

At four years old, Halsey's grandmother taught her to play piano. Her first song was "Memory" from the musical *Cats*. Soon after, the musician started playing string instruments. She asked for her own violin. But her dad thought she would lose interest. Still, her mom found her a used one. According to *Glamour*, her mom said, "We can't hold her back. We don't know what she can become." Halsey's mother always supported her art. The singer now plays eight instruments.

SINGING NONSTOP

Billie liked to sing in the bathtub. There is a home movie of two-year-old Billie singing "Twinkle, Twinkle, Little Star." "She sang nonstop, all the time," Maggie told the music site LNWY. For Billie, just like for Halsey, music was a part of her. "It's never been a question," the star told Red Bull. Music was more important than anything to the family. They had three pianos in their small house.

MAKING CONNECTIONS

At 14, Halsey picked up the guitar. However, she only started writing music at 17. It was a way to convey the poems she wrote. Singing helps her connect with the fans.

Connecting with fans is a key part of Halsey's success. Her father was a people person. Halsey learned from him. She meets many fans. The singer says she never forgets them.

EARLY SONGWRITING AND OTHER ART

Billie began writing songs at a younger age than Halsey. When she was four, she sang along with her ukulele. "I wrote a song about falling into a black hole," Billie explained to *Interview*. "But it was really upbeat." She was also interested in visual art. The singer directed movies with her friends. They used her father's digital camera. Though she went to a few auditions, Billie did not like acting. However, the star recorded background dialogue for a few movies. *Ramona and Beezus* was one.

FINDING HERSELF

The internet was important to Halsey. As a young teen, she was good at creating an online identity. She was popular on Tumblr. The soon-to-be star posted poems. Photo diaries of her adventures and sketches were posted too. "I was putting my content out there, this projection of myself," Halsey explained to *Glamour*. "I didn't know what I was doing. I was just screaming into the void." Eventually, nearly 10,000 people followed her.

HONING HER CRAFT

Halsey explored her identity online. Billie learned
music more traditionally. Her parents put her in a
group homeschool program. It was called WISH. Her
mother taught a songwriting class for WISH. In it,
Billie learned how to write songs. This is when her craft
began to catch up to her natural-born talent.

YOUTUBE STAR

YouTube was another place where Halsey expressed herself. By the time she was 18, she had 16,000 YouTube subscribers. The singer is still a big social media user. She cares about interacting with her fans. "I'm not just . . . trying to make all of these lost, misfit kids feel better," Halsey told *Rolling Stone*. "I need them to help me feel normal too."

TALENT SHOWS AND CHOIR

Billie's first performances were in homeschool talent shows. At one show, she performed a Beatles song. It was called "Happiness Is a Warm Gun." Then she joined the famous Los Angeles Children's Chorus when she was eight. Growing up, Billie also studied dance. A competitive company accepted her at 12. When she was 13, she suffered an injury. That made her stop dancing. Looking back, Billie saw that dance was always more stressful for her than singing. Both she and Halsey find comfort in their music and fans.

ANTHONY LI

One night at a party, Halsey met Anthony Li. Li played in a band called Action Item. He had heard one of Halsey's Taylor Swift covers. Then he asked her to record music for a yogurt commercial. It would pay her $500. They went to his friend's studio in New Jersey. All night, they worked on writing and recording the jingle. Later that night, Halsey wrote "Ghost." She sent it to Li. The yogurt commercial never happened. Halsey's work had Li's attention, though.

FINNEAS

Billie had help finding success too. Her brother had strong writing and production skills. He was her songwriting partner before her career began. Finneas loved Billie's voice as much as Li loved Halsey's. When they began working together, Finneas wrote most of the songs. The siblings recorded their first songs on Finneas's computer. He had bought it with his savings.

WHAT MUSIC PRODUCERS DO

A music producer is key to recording modern music. The producer has a hand in every aspect of a song or album. They might decide which instruments are played behind the singer, how many backup singers are used, and more. Sometimes the producer is also an audio engineer. That means they work on sound mixing. Producers make sure the singer and instruments sound like they should.

WHAT'S IN A NAME?

Li encouraged Halsey to come up with a new name. This would be used for performances. She came up with Halsey. This is her first name, Ashley, with the letters rearranged. Halsey is also the name of a Brooklyn subway stop she visited a lot as a teen. It isn't just a name, though. "It's . . . an amplified version of myself," she explained to music site Popjustice. "Halsey is a protagonist."

SONG STRUCTURE BASICS

Structure is important in songs. This helps the listener remember the song. It also helps them anticipate where the song might be going. A common song structure is verse / chorus / verse / chorus / bridge / chorus. The chorus is the part of the song that is the same every time. This gives the listener the big idea of the song. It's also the part that sticks in their head. Verses change through the song. They move the "story" forward. The bridge is the peak emotional moment of the song. Also, it helps bring interest and variation to the structure and listening experience.

WHAT'S IN A SONG?

The first song that Billie finished was in her mother's songwriting class. "I wrote music because I had a lot on my mind . . . and I didn't really know who to say it to," Billie said to Pigeons and Planes. "I want more people to know me so that they can feel me and relate to me."

MUSICIANS WHO STARTED YOUNG

Halsey	Was 20 when *Badlands* came out
Billie Eilish	Released *When We All Fall Asleep, Where Do We Go?* when she was 17
Shawn Mendes	Was 16 when he released his full-length album *Handwritten*
Justin Bieber	*My World 2* came out when he was 16
Miley Cyrus	Released *Hannah Montana 2*: Meet Miley Cyrus at 14
Demi Lovato	*Don't Forget* came out when she was 16
Britney Spears	*Baby One More Time* was her hit at 16
Taylor Swift	Wrote her first album *Taylor Swift* at 16

CHAPTER 3

RISE TO SUCCESS

GHOST

Halsey uploaded her song "Ghost" to SoundCloud in 2014. Her online fans spread it wide. A record label got in touch within hours. The singer asked for Anthony Li's help. He told her to use his email address. She pretended he was her manager. Li started getting emails right away. By the next morning, the two were meeting with multiple record labels. While neither of them had experience, Li soon became her actual manager.

OCEAN EYES

Finneas wrote a song called "Ocean Eyes." However, he felt his voice wasn't right for the song. Billie told *Vogue*, "He'd been doing it with his band before, but of course I'd heard it because I was right next door. I sang it, and we both loved it." The siblings recorded Billie's version of the song. Then, Finneas put a link up on SoundCloud in November 2015. They only created the link so Billie's dance teacher could download it. His plan was to have students dance to the song. Just like when Halsey uploaded "Ghost," the song gained attention rapidly.

CONTROLLING HER MUSIC

In Halsey's first meetings, labels wanted to put her "in development." They would mold her into a musician they could market. Halsey needed the money badly. But control over her music was more important. Instead of signing, she went home and wrote more music. Then, Sirius radio picked up "Ghost." Record labels again took notice. The conversation changed. "I've cultivated a fan base . . . and now it's, 'What can we do for you?'" she told Popjustice. The singer signed with Astralwerks in June 2014 for $100,000. She was only 19.

INTEREST FROM LABELS

"Ocean Eyes" wasn't the first song Billie put on SoundCloud. It was her first viral hit, though. The song became popular literally overnight. SoundCloud is where the tune was first noticed. Then it was picked up by music discovery site Hillydilly. It soon had 2.2 million SoundCloud streams. On Spotify, the song was played over 17 million times. Billie found a manager because of the single. This was soon followed by interest from major music labels.

WHAT IS SOUNDCLOUD?

Both singers started growing their fan bases on SoundCloud. This site allows users to upload, promote, and share audio recordings of their songs. SoundCloud started in 2007 and took over the part MySpace used to play in music promotion. EDM artists like Skrillex and Avicii got their start there. R&B singer Kehlani and rappers XXXTentacion and Post Malone were also discovered on SoundCloud. Established artists post new music there too.

ROOM 93

Astralwerks released Halsey's first EP in October 2014. EPs are short albums. *Room 93* was its title. The EP was written from her viewpoint of being confined to a hotel room on tour. It had five songs, including "Ghost." Halsey was a songwriter on every track. Later, she said that the album felt too safe. She was not pushing her limits. At the time, though, it did well for a debut EP.

CHOOSING A LABEL CAREFULLY

The Baird O'Connells took their time. Billie and her family met with labels for a year. Finally, they signed with an Interscope label called Darkroom. Their reasons for choosing the label were similar to Halsey's. They believed that Darkroom saw their daughter as a long-term project. She was not just a quick moneymaker. Darkroom was willing to give Billie the creative freedom she craved.

Finneas O'Connell

GROWING A REAL FAN BASE

Halsey's first tour as a major-label artist was in the fall of 2014. She joined The Kooks for a U.S. tour. This band was another Astralwerks act. Her previous shows were in small clubs. The larger tour was a step up. At the time, Halsey only had an EP out. Still, she recalls that thousands of fans sang along with her at a Lollapalooza show. Touring was as important as the internet for growing her fame.

APPLE MUSIC

Apple Music was a big part of Billie's success. In January 2016, discovery platform Platoon, now owned by Apple Music, signed her to a development deal. The following year, they featured her at SXSW. Apple Music made her their "Up Next" artist, and she was interviewed on their Beats 1 radio show. Halsey was helped by Apple too. *Badlands* single "New Americana" premiered on Beats 1. Host Zane Lowe said, "There's a new icon there."

A TOP-15 EP

Darkroom released Billie's debut EP in August 2017. It was called *Don't Smile at Me*. The record included eight songs. "Ocean Eyes" was one of them. Control over the music was as important for Billie as it was for Halsey. Most tracks were written by Billie and Finneas. Some were written by Finneas alone. He also produced every song. The EP reached the top 15 in the U.S., United Kingdom, Canada, and Australia. As of March 2019, "Ocean Eyes" had been streamed more than 275 million times on Spotify.

Justin Bieber

TOURING BIGGER AND BIGGER

Touring was key to Halsey's success. The singer toured as a co-headliner with Young Rising Sons in early 2015. A few months later, she opened for global sensation Imagine Dragons. Then, she opened for megastar The Weeknd. "If one thousand kids walk away from that show and they like me, then I did my job. And if the other 19,000 walk away going, 'I don't really get her,' that's fine too because I was still myself and it was still an entry point," the star told Popjustice.

A METEORIC RISE

Touring soon became just as important for Billie. Don't Smile at Me kicked off a world tour. Tickets sold out within an hour. It was called the Where's My Mind? Tour. The name was based on a line from her song "Bellyache." The tour ran from February to April 2018. Across the U.S. and Europe, 26 shows were played. Billie went from singing in her bedroom to singing in stadiums. "The attention doesn't scare me. Nothing really scares me, to be honest," she told NME.

AUTHENTICITY

Halsey became famous quickly. In March 2015, she was the most tweeted-about artist at the SXSW festival. Part of her success came from her realness. It also came from her commitment to fans. "I'm genuinely myself. . . . I'm not worried about staying on brand. . . . I like talking to people," Halsey told Popjustice.

INCREDIBLE TALENT

Critics say Billie has an incredible voice. It has great range and intensity. Billie's music "ooze[s] confidence and authority," says *Atwood Magazine*. Teens love her social media and stage presence. She is as authentic as Halsey. As one fan said, she's "not afraid to get a bit weird." Her persona has been described as defiant but playful. Some call her dark but laid back. All of this made her a massive star even before her first album dropped.

CAREER MILESTONES

1994
Halsey is born in New Jersey.

2001
Billie is born in Los Angeles.

2008
She begins learning guitar.

2013
She writes her first full song inspired by *The Walking Dead*.

2014
After signing with Astralwerks, her debut *EP, Room 93, is released*.

2015
Halsey releases her debut album, *Badlands,* and starts her first solo tour, which ends up selling out Madison Square Garden the following year.

2015
Finneas and Billie upload "Ocean Eyes" to SoundCloud.

2016
Billie signs a record deal with Interscope.

2017
Her album *hopeless fountain kingdom* is released and hits number one on the charts.

2017
Her debut EP, *Don't Smile at Me* is released by Interscope, launching Billie to stardom.

2019
The singer announces a third album.

2019
Her full-length album *When We All Fall Asleep, Where Do We Go?* is released. She becomes a household name.

CHAPTER 4

STARDOM

FINDING HER VOICE

In 2015, Astralwerks released Halsey's first studio album. *Badlands* was number two on the U.S. Billboard 200. The album and four singles went platinum. Her breakout single was "New Americana." This song was downloaded nearly 300,000 times by spring 2016. Halsey was very involved in writing the album. "It's kind of therapeutic for me to acknowledge that I'm living in these mental badlands," the singer told Popjustice.

AN IMPORTANT MILESTONE

Billie's music had a billion streams before she ever released an album. Her song "You Should See Me in a Crown" came out in 2018. It got more than a million streams in its first 24 hours. She also had 15 million Instagram followers. Just as they had been with Halsey, followers were drawn to Billie's realness. They also loved her edgy style. In 2018, Apple Music announced that 800,000 subscribers had pre-added her upcoming album. This was more than any other album in history.

SELLING OUT MADISON SQUARE GARDEN

Halsey's first world tour was for *Badlands*. The tour ran from September 2015 to September 2016. Stops included the Lollapalooza, Bonnaroo, and Coachella festivals. Tickets for the tour sold out quickly. Venues were upgraded to provide more room. Those seats sold out too. Her Madison Square Garden show sold out in 24 hours. It was the last show of the tour.

THE FIRST ALBUM

Darkroom wanted Billie to record her first album at a professional studio. She refused. Billie and her brother recorded and produced every song at home in his bedroom. The star sang while sitting on Finneas's bed with her legs crossed. He told *Rolling Stone,* "It's crazy. Most people need to stand and open their diaphragms, but Billie sounds amazing just slumped on the bed."

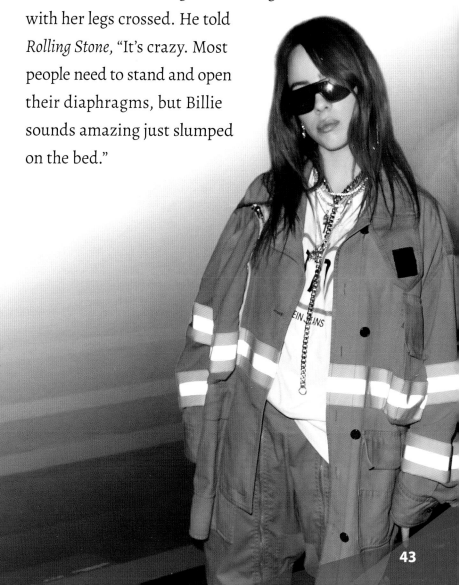

MAINSTREAM SUCCESS

In 2016, Halsey was featured on The Chainsmokers'
song "Closer." This led to major mainstream success. It
was her first number-one song on Billboard. The song
was on the top of the charts for 12 weeks. She became a
household name. "So many people attribute that song to
really important moments in their life," she told *HuffPost*.
Halsey also received her first two Grammy nominations
a few months after the song was released.

Andrew Taggart

A MASSIVE STAR

When We All Fall Asleep, Where Do We Go? debuted to massive success. Billie's first record started at the top of the Billboard 200. It returned to that spot three times before June 2019. The week her album came out, Billie had 14 songs in the top 100 on the Billboard chart. That is more than any other female artist ever. Her songs had been streamed more than 15 billion times as of September 2019.

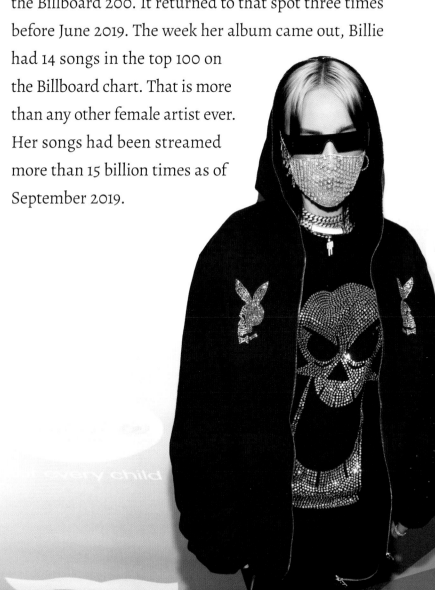

FILM-INSPIRED MUSIC

In 2017, Halsey's second album was number one. The album was titled *hopeless fountain kingdom*. It is based on purgatory and Greek myths. Director Baz Luhrmann's movie *Romeo + Juliet* inspired Halsey. This movie influenced the album's art and spoken-word tracks. Luhrmann even helped promote the album with Halsey. The singer toured for *hopeless fountain kingdom* from September 2017 to September 2018.

Baz Luhrmann

STRUGGLING WITH SUDDEN FAME

Billie became a star even faster than Halsey. Fame wasn't easy for Billie at first. The 17-year-old got rashes from exhaustion and stress. Someone leaked her address online. Fans came to the house uninvited. This made her feel unsafe. Then Billie started having nightmares. She explained to *Rolling Stone*, "I have this amazing thing in front of me, and I don't want to hate it. And I don't hate it. But I hate certain parts of it." However, her family and friends helped. Her tour schedule was reorganized so she had more days off. Friends flew in to visit with her.

WITHOUT ME

The single "Without Me" was released in October 2018. This was Halsey's first number-one solo single in the U.S. It also reached the top three in almost a dozen other countries. "Without Me" was a change for Halsey because it was a love song. Her songwriting was much more personal than before. Audiences loved it. Halsey actually replaced herself on the charts. "Eastside" overtook "Without Me" to become number one in February 2019.

INDIE POP VOICE

Both Billie and Halsey use a particular singing style and accent that is different than their speaking voice. It's known as indie pop voice. This singing style uses vocal fry, which is also described as a creaky voice. The singers pronounce vowels in a way that makes one vowel sound like two. For example, good becomes "go-oyd" and love becomes "lo-oyve." Selena Gomez also famously uses this kind of voice. Among the earliest artists to use this distinctive style were Joanna Newsom and Amy Winehouse.

Thom Yorke

ON TOP OF THE WORLD

Billie was the first artist born after the turn of the
millennium to have a number-one album. She and
Halsey each had multiple songs on the Top 100 chart in
January and February of 2019. The star went on to have
her first number-one song in August 2019. Altogether,
Billie has released six gold and three platinum singles.
Concerts have sold out around the world. Rock stars like
Dave Grohl and Billie Joe Armstrong love her music. So
does legend Thom Yorke of Radiohead. After a concert,
Billie told *Rolling Stone*, Yorke said, "You're the only one
doing anything . . . *interesting* nowadays."

COLLABORATIONS AND POLITICS

In April 2019, Halsey was featured in "Boy with Luv." The song is by Korean boy band BTS. Their single had 74.6 million views on YouTube in one day. That is the most views ever in a single day.

Halsey has also been outspoken on politics and social issues. On Earth Day in April 2019, she and 29 others were featured on a Lil' Dicky single about climate change. The single was called "Earth." Billie speaks out on politics too. In 2018 she worked with the mayor of Los Angeles to get young people to vote.

ART AND MUSIC

Visual artists have long collaborated with and influenced musicians. Takashi Murakami has worked with other musicians, such as Pharrell, on music videos. Artist Jeff Koons designed Lady Gaga's *ArtPop* cover. Drake's "Hotline Bling" video was said to be influenced by artist James Turrell. Kanye West worked with performance artist Vanessa Beecroft on the creative production of his Yeezus Tour.

Badlands

Spotify 1,545,678,000

YouTube 889,300,000

hopeless fountain kingdom

Spotify 1,267,349,000

YouTube 826,700,000

When We All Fall Asleep, Where Do We Go?

Spotify 2,142,842,000

YouTube 1,372,100,000

BECOMING A DESIGNER

Spotify set up an "enhanced album experience" for Billie in 2019. Outside was a statue of Billie. World-famous Japanese artist Takashi Murakami designed it. Inside, there were 14 rooms. Each room was for a song on the album. Workers wore white jumpsuits. The jumpsuits were from Billie's fashion line. Called Blōhsh, the line's logo is a small green stick figure. Billie began by sketching outfits herself. She still helps design a lot of the clothing. It is inspired by the singer's streetwear style.

CHAPTER 5

INFLUENCES AND COLLABORATIONS

A BLEND OF INDIE AND HIP-HOP

Halsey's father listened to hip-hop. Artists like Notorious B.I.G., Tupac, and Slick Rick were some of his favorites. Her mother played the Cure, Nirvana, and Tori Amos. Halsey loved Amos's realness and rawness. "I think music is a universal language, it's how you introduce walks of life that are not otherwise familiar to people," she told Popjustice.

Tori Amos

THE BEATLES AND AVRIL LAVIGNE

Billie was also influenced by her father's favorite music. He loved pop-punk bands and the Beatles. "My dad used to make us mixtapes of all the stuff that he liked, which was Avril Lavigne, Linkin Park, Green Day, and a ton of the Beatles—the Beatles was a huge thing growing up," said Billie to *Interview*. She still really loves the Beatles. Avril Lavigne contacted Billie after her first album was released. Avril complimented the album and offered support.

Billie Joe Armstrong

SWAGGER

Halsey has said that Kanye West, Brand New, and Bright Eyes are inspirations. She admires film directors like Quentin Tarantino and Larry Clark as well. The singer is influenced by the swagger and confidence of male musicians. "All the musicians I loved growing up were men," she said. Some of her favorites were Leonard Cohen, Mick Jagger, and Matty Healy from The 1975.

TOP BILLBOARD HOT 100 SINGLES

● HALSEY

#1	🎵	**Closer** featuring The Chainsmokers	9/2016
#5	🎵	**Bad at Love**	1/2018
#9	🎵	**Eastside** featuring Benny Blanco, Khalid	1/2019
#1	🎵	**Without Me**	1/2019
#8	🎵	**Boy with Luv** featuring BTS	4/2019

DISCOVERING HIP-HOP

Billie admires hip-hop. She loves that it is like poetry, with rhymes and references woven in. Similar to Halsey, many of her biggest influences are men. Childish Gambino's 2013 album *Because the Internet* was her introduction to rap, at age 11. Rapper Tyler, the Creator "changed the way she thinks" about music and fashion. Tyler, the Creator admires her too. He has said he would love to work with Billie.

● **BILLIE EILISH**

#14	♫	Bury a Friend	2/2019
#31	♫	Wish You Were Gay	4/2019
#29	♫	When the Party's Over	4/2019
#35	♫	Xanny	4/2019
#1	♫	Bad Guy	8/2019

Kanye West

AESTHETIC GOALS

Halsey thinks of music as a universe. She wants to transport listeners to a new world. "Kings of Leon records, Lana Del Rey records, Kanye records, Frank Ocean records . . . I go somewhere when I listen to them. Those records feel like they exist in their own dimension. They exist in a world where everything is consistent," the star said to Popjustice. The singer has used the idea of a different world in all of her albums.

OPENING UP ABOUT HEALTH ISSUES

Billie has Tourette's syndrome and Halsey has endometriosis. Each has been open about their health issues. Halsey revealed her diagnosis on Twitter. She gave a speech for the Endometriosis Foundation of America. Billie revealed her Tourette's syndrome on Instagram. This was after fans released a video of her tics. She then talked about it on *Ellen*. Billie has also been open about her history of self-harm, while Halsey does not shy away from discussing her bipolar disorder.

DANCE AND OTHER ART

Billie's dance training influences how she thinks about music. For her, a song must be danceable. Dance also helps her with her confidence and stage presence. Visual art is still an inspiration for Billie too. In her journal, Billie often sketches dark and detailed pictures. The star's notebook also contains lines from her favorite songs and early drafts of her own songs.

FEMALE ARTISTS BAND TOGETHER

Halsey has been compared to Lana Del Rey, Ariana Grande, and many other female artists. However, she does not like to compete with any of them. The singer says that female artists have to work harder to be seen as unique. "I will say one thing about my generation of artists: we are just not . . . having it. Lorde, Ariana . . . if you open any of our text messages at any given time, all of us are . . . so supportive," she told *Glamour*.

Ariana Grande

Lorde

GOTH GIRLS AND TOUGH GUYS

Billie has been compared to Halsey. Critics also see her independence and goth flavor as similar to Lorde. Male artists like Kanye West and Kendrick Lamar are other points of comparison. They have similar talent and performance skills. Billie's voice has been compared to Lana Del Rey's too.

G-Eazy

COLLABORATIONS

Halsey has worked with superstars since the beginning. In 2015, she sang on the Justin Bieber song "The Feeling." She was on PARTYNEXTDOOR's song "Damage" in 2017. The singer had massive success with her single "Him & I" with G-Eazy. It was released in 2017. "Alone," a single from *hopeless fountain kingdom*, was remixed with Big Sean and Stefflon Don in 2018. A few months later, Halsey and Khalid sang on Benny Blanco's "Eastside." The song was a top-ten single.

FAMILY TIES

Finneas tours with Billie. The devoted brother plays beats and guitar. He also harmonizes while Billie sings. Their parents go on tour too.

Although Finneas has his own house now, it's close by. His bedroom in their childhood home remains untouched. This helps maintain the music the two make together. "It's our house and it's where we live—it's where we have experienced everything," Finneas told AWAL.

SIBLING ACTS

Families often make good bands. The pop rock band Haim is made up of three sisters from Los Angeles. They grew up playing many instruments together. The sisters even played in a cover band with their parents when they were young. Country group The Band Perry is also made up of three siblings. Good Charlotte was started by twin brothers.

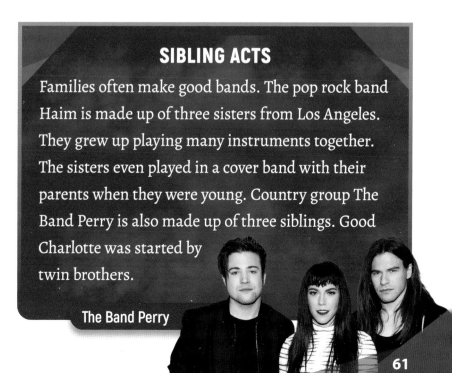

The Band Perry

Lauren Jauregui

FRIENDS AND COLLABORATORS

Former Fifth Harmony singer Lauren Jauregui is Halsey's close friend. They sang the duet "Strangers" for *hopeless fountain kingdom*. The two were together for the *hopeless fountain kingdom* tour in South America. Halsey tweeted that "Lauren is so special because best friend or not, her music would still be exactly what I need in the moment and it gives me goosebumps. It's just even better that I'm lucky enough to know and love her."

WORKING WITH IDOLS

Collaborations are important to Billie too. The song "Lovely" with Khalid was released in April 2018. Her longtime idol Justin Bieber sang a remix of Billie's single "Bad Guy" in 2019. Billie has been a fan of his for years. The art for the single featured Billie in her room with posters of Justin.

Khalid

SHARED COLLABORATIONS

Both have collaborated with Justin Bieber.

Lana Del Rey is a **shared** point of comparison.

Khalid brought **each of them** on stage at Coachella in 2019.

Billie met with **Halsey's** 13-year-old cousin as a favor to Halsey.

They've **both** played Glastonbury, Coachella, and SXSW.